One down three across

A comedy in one act

Mary Jackson

Jasper Publishing
1 Broad St Hemel Hempstead Herts HP2 5BW
Tel; 01442 63461 Fax; 01442 217102

Copyright © Mary Jackson 1996

Jasper Publishing

1 Broad Street Hemel Hempstead
Herts HP2 5BW
Tel; 01442 63461 Fax; 01442 217102

ISBN 1 874009 17 1

One down three across

A comedy in one act

CHARACTERS

P. C. Frank Johnson	Late 40's. A kind-hearted, keen, but rather pompous police officer, with serious marital problems. Next-door neighbour of Hilda Brown and the deceased, John Brown.
Hilda	40's. Plain and homely looking. Dowdily dressed. Crossword fanatic. Superficially appears rather dim, but knows exactly what she is doing.
Alice	Late 30's. Abrasive, attractive in a pale, drawn sort of way. A haughty, upper-class 'ethnic' type. A musician.
Cleaning Lady	Plump, bustling, curious.

SETTING

Time: the present. The action of the play takes place in the waiting area outside the door of what appears to be a Hospital Pathology Lab.

ONE DOWN THREE ACROSS

*Curtain Music; 'Dem Bones, Dem Bones, Dem Dry Bones'... (as required)...
Oh, hear the word of the Lord!*

*Frank enters solicitously with Hilda. He is plainly disgusted to hear the music.
The Path. Lab. door is ajar. The Cleaning Lady comes out with a large sweeping
brush. She shuts the door behind her. The music ceases abruptly, and she
shuffles off, dragging her brush.*

FRANK Sorry about that, Hilda. Very poor taste - I shall have to raise an official
voice of complaint. Use my influence. *(indicating a chair)* Now then, you sit
down and leave everything to me.

Hilda sits. Frank sits next to her

FRANK Hope it hasn't upset you too much, Hilda. The music.
HILDA Don't you worry about me, Frank. I'm all right. Although I dare say
John would have preferred 'Nessun Dorma' - y'know - the World Cup theme.
He got quite excited when that came on. *(thoughtfully)* Perhaps not. It's no
place to be getting excited, is it? Well, not in his position.
FRANK *(earnestly)* I just want to say... Well, I know it's all been a terrible
shock, Hilda, but you are not alone.

Frank is disconcerted to see Hilda rooting about in her shopping bag

FRANK No! You are not alone! I'm here with you - every step of the way.
Professionally - and, I trust - as a close friend.

*Hilda pulls out a newspaper and a biro, finds the crossword page, and begins
to study it with relish*

FRANK And you're not to worry about the... er... formalities. Not pleasant,
Hilda. Not pulling any punches. But - I'm with you. Oh, yes! *(standing,
emotional)* God! You must be going through absolute hell! I - well, I just can't
believe it's happening! Even though I was there - standing there - with him, I
just can't take it in. It's a nightmare!
HILDA One down ... eight and seven. Something something R...

FRANK *(pacing)* Trapped in a nightmare! A nightmare! That's what it is. And any minute now we'll wake up and escape from it!

HILDA *(delighted)* MERCIFUL RELEASE! *(filling in the crossword)* Now, I should be able to get one down three across! It's been driving me mad!

FRANK That car came from nowhere! There we were, the three of us, Janet, me - and John - chatting happily together outside the news-agent's. Not a care in the world. Then - just a space - on the footpath - where a friend and neighbour had stood with his newspaper tucked under his arm.

HILDA *(gleefully writing)* REVERSAL OF FORTUNE!

FRANK Snatched away. Snatched away! As if by a giant hand! But at least he went with a smile on his face. You can take comfort from that.

HILDA Did you see it, then?

FRANK The car?

HILDA The smile on his face, when he was snatched away. As if by a giant hand.

FRANK It had faded a bit, when I reached him. He was fifty yards further up the road, then, of course.

HILDA Isn't it even - a little bit lop-sided?

FRANK Ah. I can see you're worrying about the identification. Well, don't. I can assure you nothing's - lop-sided. He's just the same old John as he ever was, but - gone. And yet not gone.

HILDA *(looking up, sharply)* Four letters, Frank. D. E. A. D. If you're D. E. A. D. you can't be gone and yet not gone. It's one or the other.

FRANK *(deep sigh, patiently)* He had a good life. That's got to count for something.

HILDA Shortish, though.

FRANK Of quality, though, Hilda. Of quality. Oh, yes. You were a good wife. He had the best. Believe me, you have nothing to reproach yourself for. I envied your John, you know. I often said to him: 'Your Hilda's a wife in a million!' His reply was always the same: 'She's two in a million, is my Hilda!'

HILDA That's one thing I shan't miss, his sarcasm. 'There's another, thinner woman lurking somewhere inside you, Hilda,' he'd say, 'but she's concussed with all those roast potatoes you shovel down your throat!' Not a lot of good to say about anyone, really, when I think about it - *(pointedly)* - with one or two notable exceptions.

FRANK Yes. Well. I - I came straight for you, you know after...

HILDA He was snatched away? You said.

FRANK Know the routine, you see. Knew they'd bring him here. And I was just going off duty

HILDA You said.

FRANK The very least I could do, Hilda, in the circumstances!

HILDA Yes. It was.

FRANK Knew you'd need some strong support.

HILDA Thank you, Frank. *(small pause, pointedly)* Janet went home, then, did she? Didn't she need some strong support?

FRANK And, of course, it goes without saying that I'll stay with you until ... *(emotionally)* Oh, God! You know ... until ...

HILDA Have you got the newspaper?

FRANK What?

HILDA The newspaper. The one he'd just bought, when he was standing with you - and Janet - without a care in the world. Before he was snatched away. As if by a giant's hand. That one, Frank.

FRANK Er... Well, yes. It's in the car. I could fetch it for you.

HILDA It doesn't matter this very minute, as long as I know it's safe.

Frank, struggling with his own emotions, grips Hilda's hand fiercely in a gesture of support

FRANK Sorry, Hilda. Should have thought. Of course - the newspaper. You'll want to keep it. To cherish - as a memento of his last moments.

HILDA For last night's crossword solution, actually. *(returns to the crossword)* Note toxic gases in foreign...? Note toxic... Got it! EXOTIC! *(fills in the word, looks up brightly)* That's just reminded me. Exactly this time last year you and Janet were on holiday in Majorca! Majorca! Oh, I was green with envy! I really wanted John to lash out for once on something exotic. Not just a can of lager on the patio.

FRANK It's no trouble - if you want the newspaper.

HILDA Ooh, and that tan! Your Janet was determined to wear a bikini. And she did! Didn't she look stunning? In the photos?

FRANK The photos? Oh, you saw them, did you?

HILDA It was John who kept asking her to bring them round. He seemed to have a strange fascination for Majorca. The beach, the highrise apartment blocks - and Janet - in her little bikini. Didn't you notice?

FRANK The bikini?

HILDA John's strange fascination! For the photographs. Of Majorca.

FRANK There's nothing strange about being interested in holiday snaps, Hilda.

HILDA Ooh, but they weren't just holiday snaps were they, Frank? *(dropping her voice to a whisper)* What about - the others?

Frank looks hard at her

HILDA Just using up the roll, were you? In the bedroom, and the bathroom, and on the goat-skin rug? She came out very well. Very photogenic, your Janet. From every angle.

FRANK Oh, my God! Not those! She didn't show you...?

HILDA Oh, yes, she did! But don't panic! Not a word to anyone! She said. 'If anyone saw these, my Frank's career would be on the line! On the line!' Oh, she was very emphatic about that. Funny though. Because she must have given John one or two of them. I found them in his briefcase.

FRANK Oh, my God!

HILDA It's all right. I hid them.

FRANK I must insist you return them, Hilda. Immediately.

HILDA ...but I've forgotten where.

FRANK Oh, my God!

HILDA Well, it just didn't seem right to have pictures of a policeman's wife, you know - lying around, at funny angles like that.

FRANK Those photographs are works of art, Hilda. There's a very fine and subtle line between art - and funny angles, you understand? But - as an art connoiseur - I can assure you those photographs are masterpieces - masterpieces! - of the human form. You've only to look at Michaelangelo, Rubens, Rodin with his nudes...

HILDA And Frank Johnson's wife handcuffed naked to the billiard table? Oh, come on! Even I know pornography when I see it!

FRANK *(badly shaken)* Hilda!

They are interrupted by the wail of an ambulance siren

HILDA Trouble. For someone. *(returns to her crossword)*

Frank sits down next to her

FRANK *(taking a deep breath, solicitously)* It's very strange, you know, Hilda, the way people react to sudden bereavement. Now, for example, some people may think it's just a little bizarre to see you engrossed in a crossword outside a Mortuary. But I'd argue the point with them. Oh, yes. I would. Because - well, I think I understand what's happening to you, Hilda. You see, what you've done is fall back, psychologically speaking, on what we call familiar role play: in your case, the comfort of the crossword puzzle. But there's more to it than that. *(warming to his theme)* Oh, yes. Much more. You see, all your senses, your nerve-endings, your imagination - are all behaving wildly - capriciously - as if they've suddenly been catapulted into brilliant technicolour.

Hilda, having heard him out, goes back to her crossword. Frank puts his hand over it to hide it

FRANK Classic text-book reaction! Shock, Hilda. You are in shock. And the photographs are not pornographic!

Hilda gently picks up his hand and puts it on his lap, with a little pat

HILDA Hang on. I should be able to get this. *(reading)* 'Is this character in stripes a charlatan, perhaps, or just a sucker? Could be both!' *(smiles and looks up at Frank)* Mmm. A charlatan - in stripes!

FRANK They are not pornographic! I can assure you, Hilda, that my integrity as a photographer is beyond dispute. Just as my motives in bringing you here are beyond dispute. Straight down the line! Duty, friendship, compassion! There's nothing of the - charlatan, about my hobbies or my motives! And I resent any suggestion...

HILDA ... of a classic text-book reaction? To - guilt?

FRANK Guilt? Good God, woman! I'm not guilty of anything! Now listen to me, Hilda. I sympathise - totally sympathise - with the dreadful distress you must be feeling, but let's get this straight here and now. It was some other bastard - not me - who ran poor old John down!

HILDA Did I suggest it was you who ran poor old John down? I don't think so, Frank. I was talking about photographs. I simply suggested they were a bit... well, you know. Anyway, if you're not guilty of anything, why are you looking like a criminal? Oh, come on, Frank! Cheer up. All this - because of a crossword clue?

Alice enters. She sees Frank and Hilda but doesn't speak or acknowledge their presence. She looks at the Hospital Signs in a perplexed manner, and follows the arrows off. Frank and Hilda watch her go

FRANK Sorry, Hilda. Blew it, then, didn't I? A crossword clue! It's well, it's all this waiting around. Get's to you. Sorry. Very sorry. *(recovering)* Well, they know we're here. I 'phoned through on my mobile. We should have been called in straight away. It just isn't fair - on you. Far too stressful. I'll have a quick word with the Pathologist - you know - professionally. Get him moving. Oh, yes. He listens to me. Respects my judgement. Well, we've worked together before. I think I can safely say I've got a bit of clout around here. Crossword clue, eh? Got me going then, didn't you? *(patronising her)* And what was the answer?

HILDA HUMBUG! A sucker! A charlatan in stripes! Clever, isn't it? HUMBUG!

FRANK *(uneasily)* Very clever. Yes. You're very good at it. Very quick. I'd never have got that one. How do you do it?

HILDA Practice, Frank. Years and years of practice. A great comfort are crosswords - when you're left on your own a lot - and you get to thinking all sorts of strange thoughts. Makes things bearable. Shuts it all out.

FRANK The loneliness?

HILDA Things.

FRANK *(quietly, after a thoughtful pause)* I'm really sorry, Hilda. I thought I was acting in your best interests.

HILDA *(startled)* Did you?

FRANK Bringing you here like this. I thought it'd be all over and done with by now. Just whip you in and whip you out. Take you home, put the kettle on - do a bit of talking, over a nice cup of tea. Things you need to know. Heart-to-heart stuff. I feel as if I've let you down - badly. Anyway, I'll go and have a word with the Pathologist. Time to use a bit of professional clout, as we say. In the Force.

Frank goes over to the Path. Lab. door, knocks, opens it, and makes to go in, but stops suddenly

*MUSIC: Ko-Ko's Song from 'TRIO & CHORUS' (Gilbert & Sullivan's 'The Mikado')
is playing loudly*

> 'I seized him by his little pigtail,
> And on his knees fell he,
> As he squirmed and struggled, and gurgled and guggled,
> I drew my snicker-snee, my snicker-snee!
> Oh, never shall I forget the cry,
> Or the shriek that shriek-ed he.'

Frank slams the door shut without going in. The music ceases. He heaves a deep sigh, takes out his handkerchief and blows his nose loudly

FRANK *(emotionally)* I can't go in, Hilda! I can't face seeing poor old John on the slab! Oh, God! I'm so sorry! This is dreadful! It's well, it's got me, Hilda - *(puts his hand to his heart)* - right here!

Hilda, giving him a long look as he takes out a handkerchief and mops at his brow, returns to her crossword

The Cleaning Lady has entered with her sweeping brush, unheard and unseen by Frank and Hilda. She moves close to Hilda and listens as Hilda speaks

HILDA Five across, 'Hamming on stage perhaps?' Ten letters. An 'O' with an 'R' in the middle. Over-done? Over-cooked?

The Cleaning Lady silently mouths, 'OVERACTING.'

HILDA *(filling in the letters)* OVERACTING!

The Cleaning Lady nods and smiles over Hilda's shoulder

FRANK *(angrily)* Stop it, Hilda! That's far enough! You're making them up! You're getting at me - with stupid bloody crossword clues!

As he moves towards Hilda, he spots the Cleaning Lady and glares at her

FRANK *(officiously)* Can I help you, Madam?

She shakes her head nervously and scuttles off. She opens the Path. Lab. door. As she struggles to get the sweeping brush through the door we hear

MUSIC: 'The Sergeant's Song', 'Pirates of Penzance' - Gilbert & Sullivan.

'Oh, take one consideration with another, with another,
A policeman's lot is not a happy one,
When constabulary duty's to be done, to be done,
The policeman's lot is not a happy one, happy one!"

She gets the brush through, slams the door and the music ceases

FRANK See? Everybody's getting at me!
HILDA Everybody isn't getting at you! I certainly don't want to get at you. I just want to share things with you. We've shared such a lot over the years - wouldn't you say? Come on. Sit down.

Frank sits next to Hilda

FRANK Sorry. Very sorry, Hilda. It's not you. It's me. I just can't take it all in. Such a tragedy. Such a terrible loss. This dreadful place! There's only one comforting thought. At least - *(deep sigh)* - he didn't linger.
HILDA Well, only for fifty yards. *(thoughtfully)* Could it have been suicide?
FRANK It wasn't suicide, Hilda. It was an accident. I was there.
HILDA He had a lot on his mind. You must have noticed.

FRANK John was many things, Hilda - but I can assure you he wasn't suicidal.

HILDA May be it was - murder?

FRANK It wasn't murder, Hilda. It was an accident! Look, I know you must be searching around desperately for explanations. For some - reason. And believe me, I do understand. I really do. It's very difficult to accept sudden death. It's so - incredibly final.

The Path. Lab. door opens. Hilda and Frank watch as the Cleaning Lady struggles out with an electric floor polisher

MUSIC: Pooh-Bah's Song from Trio & Chorus, 'The Mikado', Gilbert & Sullivan

> 'Now though you'd have said that head was dead. (For its owner dead was he)
> It stood on its neck, with a smile well-bred,
> And bowed three times to me.'

She gets the machine out, closes the door and the music ceases

FRANK *(weakly)* It's a nightmare!

HILDA It certainly was for my poor husband! And I'm not being fobbed off with platitudes, Frank! I'm telling you it could have been murder! Somebody was out to get him.

Frank turns and sees the Cleaning Lady once again listening wide-eyed to their conversation. He stands, glaring at her

FRANK *(pompously)* Is there some problem, Madam?

The Cleaning Lady hurries off, dragging her floor polisher with her. Frank sits again

FRANK Nobody was out to get him, Hilda.

HILDA Oh, yes, they were! Somebody bribed all the traffic wardens for miles around. It was awful. Everywhere he parked he got a parking ticket. He ended up with dozens of them. It made him ill, it really did. Oh, you must remember! He changed the car! Different make, different colour.

FRANK Men do change their cars, Hilda. There's nothing sinister in that.

HILDA Oh, isn't there? The very next day - another parking ticket! Wouldn't you call that sinister? He was being watched, Frank! Victimised! Somebody had it in for him - with a vengeance!

FRANK Hilda, this is shock! Clinical shock, believe me. Your imagination's running away with you.

HILDA Rubbish! I distinctly heard him talking to your Janet about it one night! And that wasn't imagination! They were both very upset about those parking tickets, I can tell you! I watched them through the dining-hatch all the time I was washing-up! By the time I'd finished they both seemed to be a lot calmer. As if they'd resolved something. *(pause, with a side-ways glance at Frank)* I think they'd sorted out who the somebody was.

FRANK *(alarmed)* Did they - mention a name?

Hilda moves to the table with her newspaper, watched by Frank. As she speaks she folds it into a hat

HILDA At times John could be very protective. He just said - a few days later - that I could stop worrying. There'd been no more parking tickets. The vendetta was over. So, strictly speaking, I never knew who'd been responsible. Well - not exactly.

FRANK Not - exactly. *(recovering)* Ah. I see. Well, he should have had a word with me, Hilda. Professionally. I'd have got to the bottom of it. Can't have a man hounded like that.

HILDA Well, it was very difficult, Frank. You see, from what I overheard, it appeared that the somebody responsible was living very close to us. A neighbour. A friend, in fact.

Frank's hands start shaking - violently. Hilda sees them

FRANK *(jumping up)* All this hanging about! It's ridiculous! Where's that bloody Pathologist?

Frank moves to the Path. Lab. door

HILDA My hands were shaking just like that last night.

Frank rams his hands into his pocket

HILDA You see, I started filling in the crossword as usual, but after I'd filled in one or two clues, a bit uneasily I must say - well, I started to get suspicious. Oh, I'd been well and truly caught out! Well! It wasn't the regular, was it? My hands shook like trees in the wind!

FRANK *(disparagingly)* Someone else setting the crossword upset you that much?

HILDA It most certainly did! It's an awful shock to find out you're not half as clever as you think you are. I've had a lot of time to study people's quirks and foibles, with John being away so much. And Janet always being around when he was at home. Until the parking ticket fiasco, that is. She stopped coming round after that night. She never said why. Just never set foot in the house ever again.

FRANK *(quickly)* The crossword. You were saying?

HILDA Oh, yes. Well, I pulled myself together. 'Oh, come on, Hilda,' I thought. 'Get your white blobber out. Cover up your mistakes!' So I did! I blobbed them out! I've got very crafty over the years. Devious, I think you'd say.

FRANK *(brightly patronising)* I wouldn't say a white blobber made you devious and crafty, Hilda. Quite the opposite. Simply prepared for mistakes! Oh, yes! I'd say it proves you're a very open sort of person. Open - and honest.

The sound of an electric floor polisher interrupts him

(raising his voice as it gets nearer) In fact, going back to what we were saying, I think if you'd known who was setting John up - with the Traffic Wardens - assuming someone was, of course then you'd have told me.

Frank, exasperated, walks to one side of the stage to check the noise. As he does so, the Cleaning Lady enters from the other side, dragging the floor polisher. He doesn't notice Hilda put the newspaper hat on her head. The Cleaning Lady stops, turns off the machine, and stares curiously at Hilda. Frank sees her and takes a purposeful step towards her, with a baleful look. At the same time an Ambulance siren wails

HILDA Trouble for someone.

The Cleaning Lady scuttles off with the polisher

FRANK *(returning to Hilda)* You would tell me, wouldn't you? *(sees the hat)* Good God, Hilda! What on earth are you doing with that paper on your head?

Hilda picks up a magazine from off the table and pretends to read it like a charge sheet

HILDA *(solemnly intoning)* The charge before us today is that P-C. Frank Johnson caused serious mental anguish to the deceased, John Brown, by bribing Traffic Wardens to book him at every opportunity.

FRANK Oh, come on!

HILDA Sit down! Or you'll be done for contempt!

Frank sits, looking rather stunned

HILDA Thank you. *(reading again)* Not only that: there may well be another far more serious charge laid against him in a higher court: that of shoving the deceased just before he was deceased straight under the wheels of a car! Outside a news-agents.

FRANK You've lost your marbles, woman!

HILDA Oh, yes. And taking pornographic pictures of his wife.

FRANK You're stark raving mad!

HILDA Does the prisoner plead guilty or not guilty?

Frank jumps up, extremely agitated

FRANK Guilty of what? You're a candidate for bloody Broadmoor, you are!

HILDA *(putting down the magazine)* Bribery? Murder? Pornography? Start where you want, Frank. But I want the truth - the whole truth - about you - and Janet - and John.

FRANK *(shouting)* There's nothing to bloody tell!

HILDA *(quietly)* If you carry on insulting my intelligence you'll leave me with no choice but to take those photographs to your Superior Officer.

FRANK Good God, woman! You can't do that! It'd be the end of my career! For crying out loud, Hilda! We've been friends and neighbours for years! Doesn't that mean anything to you? What about poor old John - lying dead - in there! For Christ's sake, let him rest in peace!

HILDA I'd like to rest in peace too, Frank - whilst I'm still breathing! I want to know exactly what was going on.

FRANK Hilda!

HILDA The truth, Frank. Or else. Start with the parking tickets.

FRANK *(sitting, quietly)* You want the truth?

Hilda nods

FRANK The truth is that your husband and my wife were driving me crazy. I just couldn't cope with their - relationship.

HILDA Affair, Frank. Oh, it's all right. You can say it: my husband and your wife were having an affair.

FRANK You knew? Then why this charade?

HILDA Because I didn't know for sure, and I had to. It's been tormenting me - like a word in a crossword puzzle. Afraid? Affirm? Affair? Well, it turned out to be affair. The puzzle's almost solved. And the parking tickets?

FRANK I thought they'd scare him off - and they did. He guessed it was me, the long arm of the law! Hilda, I'm so sorry, and very ashamed. It all seems so childish now. *(hesitantly)* There is - well, there is something else. Something you need to know. But not now. We're neither of us in any state to handle it - not here - not in this place. We'll talk later. Alright? Friends?

Hilda nods. Alice enters

FRANK *(taking off Hilda's hat)* You don't need this, then.

Alice is startled to see Frank taking the paper hat off Hilda's head, but carries on walking, turning her head to watch them. Hilda straightens out the newspaper

FRANK *(jumping up)* Can I help?
ALICE *(without pausing, exits)* I very much doubt it.

Frank sits down again

HILDA *(to Frank, in a loud whisper)* 'WEARING-A-GUN.'
FRANK *(jumping up)* Good God! Is she?
HILDA *(indicating the crossword)* Seven-two-four. 'DRESSED TO KILL!' That got you, didn't it?

Frank snatches the newspaper off HILDA and crushes it

FRANK No more crosswords, Hilda!

As Hilda good-naturedly attempts to snatch it back, Alice returns. They see her and Frank lets go. Hilda straightens out the paper

FRANK *(to Alice)* Crossword fanatics! Really gets you!
ALICE I've been following arrows for miles! I assume this must be the Waiting Room?
FRANK Yes. Yes, it is. Please. Come and sit down.

Frank offers the chair next to Hilda. Alice sits, leaving a gap, and Frank sits in the middle of the two women. There is an uncomfortable silence

FRANK *(to Alice)* Sudden bereavement?

ALICE *(stiffly)* Very sudden.

FRANK My condolences. Husband?

ALICE It's disgraceful, isn't it? There must be hundreds of miles of corridors in this place! How long have you been waiting?

FRANK Quite a while.

ALICE It's like a bus station.

FRANK There seems to be some sort of hold-up.

ALICE Well, I don't intend to sit here queueing for the rest of the day. There must be somebody who knows what's going on.

HILDA *(pointing to the Path.Lab. door)* I think there's someone in there.

Frank looks hard at Hilda. Alice goes to the door, knocks, and opens it without waiting

MUSIC: a few bars of: 'John Brown's body lies a mouldering in the grave.'

Alice, shocked, slams the door shut and stands with her back to it, breathing deeply

FRANK *(to Hilda)* Satisfied?

HILDA She deserved it! What a snob!

FRANK That I told you the truth - about the parking tickets? And that you'll keep it strictly between the two of us?

HILDA There's just one other thing. *(accusingly)* Fluffy!

FRANK *(taken aback)* Fluffy?

HILDA Fluffy!

FRANK What about Fluffy?

HILDA Every time you've gone away I've loooked after Fluffy. And then - last Christmas - into kennels! No explanation. Just told. She's going in kennels! Oh, Frank, I was so hurt. What had I done to offend you?

FRANK Nothing! Nothing at all! It wasn't my doing, Hilda, I assure you.

Alice takes a seat, leaving Frank between the two women

ALICE I'm in no rush, really.

The three sit once again in an uncomfortable silence. The sound of an ambulance can be heard

HILDA Ooh, that dreadful sound. Makes me shiver. It always means trouble for some poor soul.

Alice and Frank stare fixedly ahead. Hilda shrugs, straightens the crumpled paper as best she can, and looks at the crossword

HILDA *(with a deep sigh)* I just can't get one down three across!
FRANK *(to Alice)* Crossword addict.

Alice, unimpressed, smiles patronisingly at Frank, who smiles nervously back at her

FRANK Yes! Well! How about if I go and find you ladies a nice cup of tea? There's a W.V.S. stall back down there.
HILDA What a good idea! I could murder a chocolate biscuit or a bit of fruit cake.
FRANK *(brightly)* Anything to please a lady! *(to Alice)* What can I bring you? I'm sorry, I didn't catch your name.
ALICE Coffee. De-caffeinated. Thank you.

Frank makes to leave, but comes back to Hilda, and whispers in her ear

FRANK What we were saying, Hilda. I'm very sorry you were upset. We were both victims. You and me. You do understand? All forgiven? Right! A nice cup of tea!
HILDA And a bit of fruit cake.

Frank exits

HILDA *(to Alice)* Does it taste the same?
ALICE I beg your pardon?
HILDA De-caffeinated. Does it taste the same? As ordinary?
ALICE Yes.
HILDA Oh.
ALICE But far healthier.
HILDA Fancy that. *(pause)* Your husband, did you say?
ALICE I didn't. But it is.
HILDA Didn't keep him too healthy, then.
ALICE *(icily)* He didn't die from lack of caffeine.
HILDA What did he die from lack of? If you don't mind me asking.
ALICE *(angrily)* He didn't die from lack of anything!

HILDA Oh. *(pause)* Just breath.

ALICE What?

HILDA Lack of breath. He died from. You can't die from nothing.

Alice glares ahead. Hilda returns to her crossword

ALICE I didn't mean to snap at you. I'm - distraught.

HILDA That's alright. I'm distraught, too.

ALICE Just a police car, a stranger's knock on the door, and suddenly - one is a widow.

HILDA Exactly the same for me! Except that the knock on the door was Frank, my next door neighbour, the one whose just gone for the tea. He thought he'd save me all the trauma, bringing me straight here. Very kind. Very conscientious, too. He studies a lot, you know. Wants to better himself. Be a detective. Have you got somebody?

ALICE Sorry?

HILDA Family. Or friend. To wait with you?

ALICE They're coming up from London. A young police-woman offered, but I couldn't cope with all that patronising compassion.

HILDA She'll be in there now. *(indicating Path. Lab. door)* The young police-woman. They have to watch while the pathologist... Oh, it's dreadful for them. Their eyes go all glassy and then they just slowly slump to the floor. They get used to it, eventually. Hardened, you know. But at first... Oh, I've seen it happen, many times.

ALICE *(surprised)* Oh! You're a pathologist, are you?

HILDA On telly.

ALICE *(frostily)* Oh, I see. We don't own a television.

HILDA Mine loved his telly. He was away a lot, on business, but he knew all the programmes. As soon as he came through the door: 'Turn that box on, Hilda! Let's forget the troubles of the day!' And if I gave him steak pudding and chips on his knee...! 'This is Heaven, Hilda!' he'd say. 'Or as close as a man can get to it on this earth!'

ALICE Heart-attack, I presume.

HILDA Car accident.

ALICE How old was he?

HILDA Forty seven.

ALICE So was mine. But I think you'll find that yours will have had a heart-attack at the wheel. I'm not criticising you personally, you understand - I wouldn't be so unkind - in the present circumstances, I mean - but - well, cholesterol is a killer.

HILDA Cholesterol?

ALICE We went vegetarian some years ago. I only ever buy organic fruit and vegetables. The body is a temple, a shrine, you see, and not a garbage disposal unit. Bodies should be treated with respect and reverence.

HILDA Take a lot of boiling, though, don't they?

ALICE Boiling?

HILDA Chick peas.

ALICE *(haughtily)* We don't live entirely on chick peas.

HILDA Yuk! All that lettuce and lentil stuff. Give me fish and chips out of a newspaper any day!

ALICE And look where it's got you!

HILDA The same place as you! The Mortuary!

ALICE You know what I mean. your husband. In there. Most probably because of a heart-attack.

HILDA And yours? Green-fly?

ALICE *(angrily)* Look, unlike you, I don't wish to be deliberately offensive, but quite frankly I'd prefer not to talk. I need time to think.

HILDA *(pause)* Sometimes it's better to talk. Thoughts have a way of jumping about all over the place and getting twisted and sort of snagged. But words are solid. I like words. They make things real.

ALICE *(softer)* I always did my best for him. Always. But when he was away on business he ate - garbage. I know he did! I - I found Kentucky Fried Chicken cartons in the glove compartment. Several times.

HILDA Oh.

ALICE And plastic forks.

HILDA Oh, dear.

ALICE I worked very hard to keep him healthy. We jogged. We worked out at a gymnasium. We did - all the right things. And then he'd go off on business...

HILDA And eat garbage?

Alice sniffs her acknowledgement

HILDA You'll miss him.

Alice sniffs again. Hilda looks at her keenly

HILDA No, I'm not sure, either. You see, I only ever had half of him. Three days one week, and four days the next. More like a lodger than a husband, to be honest.

ALICE I know exactly what you mean. Four days one week and three days the next in my case.

HILDA I wanted to scream some nights, when that telly went on. I wanted to talk. I wanted to know what he'd been doing. Who he'd seen. You know, feel part of his life. I only ever felt - well, sort of insignificant. And very lonely. Wasn't much of a marriage, really.

ALICE *(pause)* You're right - It is good to talk - Puts things in perspective.

HILDA Mmm.

ALICE I was a musician. A 'cellist. There was nothing else in my life before... Only my music. I wasn't attractive - to men. My sisters, though, were pretty, and married young, but I didn't envy them. Not one bit! I had my 'cello and my music! When they teased me, I'd say 'Not for me, thank you! The last thing I need is a husband! My career is far too important!' And then they, with their babes in their arms and their doting husbands at their sides, would chorus: 'Look what you're missing! Oh, you'll regret it later on!' I could laugh at them, then, and I did. I had my dreams! I had so much passion! *(reflectively, after a pause)* So much passion. *(pause)* It's an awful moment, you know, the day you wake up and realise you're nothing more than run-of-the-mill. A second-rater. Do you play?

HILDA I learned the piano when I was little but even my scales were run-of-the-mill. I've always been a second-rater. *(pause)* I'm pretty good at crosswords, though. I'm happy when I'm doing them.

ALICE Believe me, it's far better being a happy second-rater than a broken-hearted mediocrity!

HILDA Better to have had a dream than never had a dream at all.

The two women sit silently for a moment or two, deep in thought. Hilda looks down at her crossword.

ALICE I've embarassed you. I'm sorry. Wallowing in self-pity. Boring, isn't it?

HILDA No! No! It's not boring. It's just that - well, I think I've lost the art of real conversation, after all these years.

Hilda folds the newspaper and puts it decisively down on the floor

ALICE You're not just saying that - to be kind?

HILDA No! I'm not! Please go on! It's wonderful - having someone who wants to talk to me! Even in this place!

ALICE Well, the truth is that I just couldn't handle my sisters' teasing from then on. They seemed to be gloating. You know, the smug 'I told you so' look? They enjoyed - really enjoyed - being right. Seeing me left with nothing. No more dreams of immortality! It was so cruel. And incredibly painful. *(pauses, hurt by the memory)* And then... *(pulling herself together, brightly)* - he came along. He was waiting for me after a concert. Flattering, charming, and very persuasive. Oh, I willed myself to love that man! May be I did. Anyway, when he proposed, I accepted. It was the original whirl-wind romance! He even arranged for us to be married - secretly - at Gretna Green! Can you imagine anything more romantic? Can you imagine anything more satisfying than telling my family? It was my turn to gloat!

HILDA One in the eye for them! You had it all then, didn't you? Your husband and your music.

ALICE Well, actually, I gave up the 'cello. He insisted on it. Said he was afraid of losing me to a handsome violinist! Oh, it was no great sacrifice! In fact, it was very flattering - I was loved and wanted! And in front of my family I could hold my head up high again. You can't begin to understand how pathetically grateful I was. I built up an image of blissful domesticity, and I was jolly good at it, too. I fooled everyone, including myself. *(small pause, softer)* Until last year, that is, when I found out that he was - having an affair.

HILDA Good Lord! So was mine! He fell for Frank's wife - the one whose gone for the tea. Jezebel! It all started after she'd been to Majorca last year. You should have seen that tan! And there were no strap marks - know what I mean? Well, it was just like Jekyll and Hyde! She set off pale and mousy and came back tanned and erotic.

ALICE *(correcting her)* Exotic.

HILDA Exotic?

ALICE You mean tanned and exotic.

HILDA Tanned - and erotic! I know exactly what I mean! Every time my husband was home, she ran round with the holiday snaps and they'd settle down on the sofa with them. And I'd set up the Scrabble board, and sit there rattling the little letter bag at them - you know - the one you put the little wooden squares in? And then it'd be bedtime and I'd still be rattling the little letter bag. 'Oh, dear!' she'd simper. 'Just look at the time! Majorca's monopolised the whole evening yet again!' And hubbie'd laugh and say: 'Well, we've not been bored, have we, Hilda?' And I'd say: 'No, it's been absolutely fascinating.' And he'd say: 'You get off to bed, my love. You look worn out. We'll pack away the Scrabble. I'll be up soon!' Oh, I could kick myself for being so stupid!

ALICE And was he? Up soon?

HILDA I don't know. I'd drop off to sleep doing the crossword.

ALICE and **HILDA** Men!

ALICE And now...

HILDA They're both - in there.

ALICE Meeting their Maker.

HILDA Making their excuses!

ALICE Lying through their teeth!

ALICE and **HILDA** The bastards!

The two women giggle, a little shame-faced at first. Frank returns with plastic cups of tea, coffee, biscuits. He stops for a moment, startled to hear them

HILDA Wouldn't I just love to be a fly on the wall and hear him whinging and whining his excuses!
ALICE Wouldn't I just love to float past him on a cloud, playing my 'cello - with the handsome violinist turning my music for me!
HILDA 'Hell hath no fury...
ALICE 'Like a woman scorned!'

This time the women laugh wholeheartedly

FRANK *(stiffly, reprovingly)* Here you are, Hilda. Tea and digestives. No cake left, I'm afraid.
HILDA (trying to be serious) Thank you, Frank.
FRANK *(to Alice)* Sorry, I don't know your name.
ALICE *(stifling a giggle)* De-caffeinated. Thank you - Frank!

Frank sits, puzzled and uneasy. The women sip their drinks and then start giggling again

FRANK Look, have I missed something? What's the big joke?

The women smother their giggles, but don't reply

FRANK Look! I don't know what's going on, but I can tell you I don't find it in the least bit amusing! This whole bloody affair has been a nightmare!

The women's burst of laughter enrages him even more

FRANK I can live without this, you know. Good God! Where's your sense of decency?

The two women become almost hysterical with laughter

FRANK *(jumping up)* Right! That's it! I'm going to get things moving. We've all had enough of this!

Frank goes to the Path. Lab. door, knocks loudly, looks back pompously at the women, and opens the door

MUSIC: 'RIGHT SAID FRED': *Music: Ted Dicks. Words: Myles Rudge.*

> 'Right' said Fred, 'Both of us together, one each end and
> steady as we go.'
> Tried to shift it, couldn't even lift it, we was getting nowhere,
> And so we had a cuppa tea and....

Frank slams the door shut. The music ceases

FRANK   Tea break.

The women are almost hysterical with laughter

FRANK   *(moving to them, angrily)* Stop it! Stop it this instant!

The women stop abruptly

FRANK   *(sits down)* That's better. *(pauses, composing himself)* Sorry I had to shout, ladies. No choice. Straight out of the Training Manual. Hysteria. That's what it is. Hysteria. Understandable in the circumstances. Very sorry. Had to use harsh tactics.

HILDA   That's all right, Frank. No need to apologise. *(to Alice, very seriously)* He's right. It is pretty hysterical, isn't it?

ALICE   *(nodding, seriously)* On the whole - I'd say it's - pretty hysterical.

FRANK   You two are taking the bloody mickey...

HILDA   *(to Frank, interrupting)* Where did you disappear to? I thought you'd got lost.

FRANK   I - er - I rang home.

HILDA   To see if Janet was O.K.?

ALICE   *(sitting upright, suddenly alert)* Janet?

FRANK   Janet's my wife.

ALICE   Janet? Not - Jezebel?

HILDA   *(to Frank)* And was she? O.K.?

FRANK   Oh, she was fine!

ALICE   *(to Frank)* Excuse me, but I need to get this absolutely correct. Janet is your wife, is she? And you - are Frank?

FRANK   Yes. We're Hilda's next-door-neighbours.

ALICE   *(to Hilda)* Who, then, is Jezebel?

HILDA *(to Alice, hissing)* His wife! Janet!

FRANK Not for much longer! Says there's nothing worth hanging around for now John's - gone. Wants a divorce.

ALICE *(to Frank)* Have you got a dog called Fluffy?

HILDA Fluffy?

FRANK *(startled)* Well, yes. We have. But - how do you know?

ALICE Well, if you're Frank, and your wife's Janet, then I'm the lady who looked after Fluffy when you went to your mother-in-law's last Christmas.

HILDA *(turning angrily on Alice)* You looked after little Fluffy? A vegetarian? *(to Frank)* Oh, Frank! How could you? You told me she was going in kennels! It spoilt my Christmas, thinking of her all on her own! Cold and neglected!

ALICE There's no need to take that attitude! I didn't want the smelly little creature! John almost threw her through the door. 'Look after this, will you?' he said. 'A favour for Frank - a valuable client. Got to keep him sweet!' And I believed him! Until I found photographs of the valuable client's wife - Janet! - hidden in his briefcase!

FRANK Oh, God! No!

HILDA *(steely-eyed)* And did you get the funny plants to water, too?

ALICE Funny plants?

HILDA They're called cannabis something or other, aren't they, Frank? *(to Alice)* Some sort of Latin name. Pretty little yellow flowers. He promised me a cutting for the garden, but he never gave me one. Cut them all up and dried them in bunches in his airing cupboard.

ALICE Oh, did he now? But no, I didn't get the funny plants. Just Fluffy - and the funny photographs.

FRANK *(hoarsely)* Oh, God! No!

HILDA He says they're artistic.

ALICE I've seen more art in a crab-louse!

FRANK *(jumps up)* Oh, shut up, you stupid bloody cow! I've had enough of this!

Frank almost runs towards the Path. Lab. door, and throws it open

MUSIC: THEME from the film 'JAWS'

He stops mid-stride, listens, turns towards the women with a glazed expression, and stands for a moment struggling to compose himself. Then he slams the door shut. The music ceases. He returns to his chair, looking faint and shocked

ALICE *(to Hilda)* Alice. My name is Alice.

FRANK *(shocked whisper)* Alice? John's Alice?

ALICE *(to Frank)* John's Alice.

HILDA *(accusingly, to Frank)* How come Alice got Fluffy?

FRANK Bugger Fluffy! Somebody tell me I'm going to wake up!

HILDA *(to Alice, with dawning realisation)* Just a minute! Did you say: 'John - threw Fluffy through the door?' John? And you found funny photographs in his briefcase? And he just died? And he's - in there? What's your surname?

FRANK Oh, God! Why couldn't the bloody car have got me? *(faintly, to Hilda)* I wanted to spare you this, Hilda. Believe me, I really did. That's why I rushed you here. Look, there's no easy way around this. I'd better introduce you two. Hilda Brown - meet Alice Brown.

The two women shake hands across Frank

HILDA and **ALICE** How d'y'do?

They remain holding hands for a long moment, staring at each other, and thinking very hard. They unclasp hands

HILDA and **ALICE** Oh, my God!

HILDA Monday to Thursday.

ALICE Friday to Sunday!

HILDA Friday to Sunday.

ALICE Monday to Thursday!

HILDA and **ALICE** Oh, my God!

ALICE Middle name?

HILDA Kenneth. After his father!

ALICE Big mole on his...?

HILDA Yes!

ALICE Black hair on his head, but ginger...

HILDA Everywhere else!

HILDA and **ALICE** Oh, my God!

ALICE When?

HILDA 28th May, '74. I wore white. With freesias and maiden-hair fern.

ALICE 23rd August, '84. I wore a rainbow-coloured ethnic skirt and a rose in my hair.

HILDA Very pretty.

ALICE I thought so.

HILDA and **ALICE** Oh, my God!

ALICE '74! You're the real wife!

HILDA '84! You're the bigamist!

HILDA and **ALICE** The bastard!

This time their laughter completely overwhelms them

FRANK *(hoarsely, hysterically, to himself)* Hysterical! We're all hysterical! Now then, Frank! Use your training! You can handle this! Yes! Yes! It's all coming back to me! I can see the page in the Training Manual. Page 83. Page 83. Page 83!

HILDA *(slaps him round the face)* Sod Page 83! You've known about this all along, haven't you? Now talk!

FRANK I have a right to silence!

HILDA Bullshit!

FRANK I need to speak to my solicitor!

HILDA So do I! Don't forget I've still got your photographs!

FRANK Hilda! I thought we were friends!

HILDA Talk!

FRANK *(jumps up, moves off angrily)* Jack the bloody Ripper had more compassion than you two! I'm going!

HILDA *(calling after him)* The photographs, Frank!

ALICE The funny plants?

FRANK *(stops, in a turmoil)* You...! Give me a moment! Just give me a moment! *(paces, emotional)* All right! All right! Well, it all started a couple of years ago when I missed getting a promotion for the second time. There it was - the writing on the wall, 'Frank Johnson is never ever going to make it!'

HILDA and **ALICE** Aah!

Hilda pretends to bow a violin, humming 'Dee dee dee, de dee dee dee.' Alice joins in and pretends to strum a 'cello

FRANK *(louder, above the humming)* Oh, God! I couldn't sleep. I couldn't eat. I couldn't concentrate - on anything. Particularly well, marital things. You know. Bedroom things. You don't need me to spell it out. But Janet was - well, as demanding and voracious as ever.

Frank stops, deep in melancholic thought. The women stop 'playing'

HILDA *(prompting)* Janet's appetite...? Frank?

ALICE As voracious as ever?

FRANK *(angrily)* And mine wasn't! Is that what you want to hear?

HILDA So you thought you'd tickle it up a bit? With photos?

FRANK Yes!

ALICE And a little relaxing smoke?

FRANK Now and again.

HILDA But it didn't work?

FRANK No! It didn't bloody work!

HILDA So that's when Janet made a bee-line for my John?

ALICE Our John!

HILDA Our John! *(to Frank)* And you found out? And decided to frighten him off with the parking tickets.

ALICE Parking tickets?

HILDA Set all the traffic wardens on him for miles around. To frighten him off. Wheel clamps, fines, y'know. Despicable, wasn't it?

ALICE *(to Frank)* Is this true?

FRANK *(nods, miserably)* And that didn't work either! Or rather, it worked too bloody well!

As he continues, the Cleaning Lady appears with the floor-polisher in tow, unseen by them. She listens intently

FRANK Your bloody husband - besotted with my wife and terrified of losing her - broke down and confessed everything! About his other home on the other side of town! And his other wife! Oh, yes! I'd been so bloody clever with the parking tickets, I blew the whole thing sky high! He couldn't handle it! Pushed him over the top!

ALICE and **HILDA** You - monster!

FRANK And then dear Janet had got both of us - me and John. By the short and bloody curlies! A bigamist lover - and a corrupt policeman husband!

The Cleaning Lady, anxious not to miss anything, moves closer, dragging the floor polisher. They hear her and turn on her. She scuttles past them towards the Path. Lab. door, and goes straight in without knocking. There is no music. The door closes behind her and the polisher. They turn back round in unison

FRANK She told me the affair was over! It was a pack of lies! Said I'd terrified him into submission! He didn't want her any more! Oh, it was a wonderful performance! You should have seen her weeping and wailing! And then she said it had just been a sort of summer madness. It was me she really loved. Could I ever forgive her? I said of course I could, and she agreed never to go round to Hilda's ever again.

ALICE She didn't need to, did she? She just carried on - with my husband!

HILDA Our husband! At least you got poor Fluffy!

FRANK Then, about three weeks ago, she got frisky - you know - and well, I couldn't...

ALICE *(frostily, to Hilda)* Poor Fluffy? Fluffy was treated very well! I bought soya mince from the Health Food Shop! And cubed and shaped Tofu!

FRANK So she rolled us a smoke - got out the photographs and the duty-free Pernod...

HILDA *(to Alice)* Yuk! I bet she got diarrhoea!

FRANK But I still couldn't - you know, Oh, God, I'm so ashamed! She started getting nasty...

ALICE She certainly did not get diarrhoea!

FRANK ...making comparisons - with John. 'That's all in the past, Janet,' I said. 'You haven't got John now!' And she said: 'That's where you're wrong, Frank. I've had him all along, and he's twice - three times! - the man you are! He keeps me and two wives very happy! He's a real stud!'

The two women suddenly realise what Frank has just said, and turn on him, astounded. As they continue with the following dialogue, the Cleaning Lady comes out of the Path. Lab. door with a damp cleaning cloth unnoticed by them. She listens wide-eyed, and continues to listen as she wipes the 'Path. Lab.' sign. She stands back, looking puzzled, looks over to the 'Domestics' sign, realises they are in the wrong positions, and exchanges the two signs. The 'Domestics' arrow now points to the 'Path. Lab' door

HILDA and **ALICE** What! What did you just call him?

FRANK *(miserably)* A stud.

The two women laugh uproariously. The Cleaning Lady goes off, through the 'Domestics' door

ALICE *(incredulous)* A stud?

HILDA What a whopper!

ALICE The lie, you mean? Not...?

HILDA Definitely not!

FRANK You mean he wasn't...?

HILDA and **ALICE** A stud? Never! Not in a month of Sundays!

FRANK *(smilng)* You don't know how good that makes me feel! She called him 'Hot Pants' you know! Your John!

HILDA *(shrieking with laughter)* Hot Pants!

ALICE They must have been Janet's!

HILDA They couldn't have been John's!

FRANK *(laughing with them)* I'm feeling better every minute!

ALICE Taking everything into consideration, I'd say all three of us have been more sinned against than sinning, wouldn't you?

HILDA and **FRANK** Too true!

ALICE *(to Hilda)* Look, I've got an idea! What would you like to do most in the world, Hilda, when this - mess - is all over?

HILDA *(small pause, wistfully)* Go on holiday. I've never had a holiday. Somewhere exotic, I think. Like Majorca. That's the first prize for the crossword this week, Y'know. I only need one down three across! Ah, well! *(sighs deeply)*

ALICE But surely there'll be insurance money?

HILDA Oh, yes! He was well insured!

ALICE Well, there's nothing to stop you, then!

HILDA But what about you, Alice? You won't get insurance money, will you? Or widow's pension?

ALICE I don't need money. Family, you know. An aunt here, a cousin there. I'm - comfortable. All I want - desperately! - is to keep them from knowing how stupid I've been. I want them to see the tragic widow - in simple, but exquisitely tailored black - palefaced, gaunt-eyed with grief. Her beloved husband - snatched away...

HILDA As if by a giant's hand! Gone - and yet not gone!

ALICE Exactly! So this is what I suggest: you identify John, and sign all the necessary papers, and I'll have the body for the funeral! I keep my dignity in front of my dreadful family - and you claim all the insurance monies and go off to Majorca.

HILDA But what will I say - if someone asks what I've done with him?

ALICE Funeral absolutely private - at his own request! Ashes scattered - oh, scatter them anywhere you fancy!

HILDA I wouldn't want to miss the funeral, though. Not altogether.

ALICE You come as my dearest friend! We can weep over the grave together! Support each other in our mutual grief!

HILDA Oh, I don't know. *(to Frank)* You're the expert, Frank. Can we get away with this?

FRANK *(drawing himself up, officiously)* Ladies, you can't do this. Oh, no! There's been a very serious offence committed. Very serious indeed.

HILDA As serious as bribing Traffic Wardens?

ALICE And taking funny pictures?

HILDA And growing funny plants?

FRANK But with my specialist knowledge, I think I may be able to help. Oh, yes! I'm sure I can! But we'll need to talk - privately.

HILDA You could all come to my place!

ALICE Better at mine! No - 'Jezebel' - next door!

FRANK She's probably gone already!

HILDA *(wistfully)* I bet I could afford a Computerised Word Searcher as well as a holiday with all that insurance money.

ALICE Oh, Hilda, you're not going to need a Word Searcher! We're merry widows now! We've got a lot of living to make up for haven't we, Frank? I'll cook my special nut roast! And a bottle - several bottles! - of the best French wine! You do drink, Frank, do you?

FRANK *(raising a beaker)* 'To the merry widows! Long may they live!' And - ladies - may I suggest we make it three - for Majorca?

The three stand quickly in unison

HILDA and **ALICE** Viva Espana!

The three make to exit

HILDA *(turning back)* Hang on! My crossword!
ALICE and **FRANK** *(grabbing her)* Forget it!

They exit, laughing, as the the Cleaning Lady comes out of the 'Domestics' door. She is going off duty and has her hat and coat on. She is carrying a shopping bag and a ghetto blaster. She puts down the ghetto blaster, picks up Hilda's newspaper and finds the crossword

CLEANING LADY Now, what did she say? One down three across. *(reads)* 'Stamped furtively with a priceless Penny Black, mail could cause great distress.' Well, that's plain enough! BLACKMAIL! *(stands, popping the newspaper into her shopping bag. To audience)* A holiday in Majorca! Shame to waste it, don't you think? *(turns on the ghetto blaster)*

MUSIC: 'MY WAY' (Lyrics: Paul Anka)

As she exits, she sings with it, loudly, tunelessly, exuberantly. The music increases in volume until, as the curtain falls, it fills the theatre

> 'I've loved, I've laughed and cried, I've had my fill, my
> share of losing.
> And now, as tears subside, I find it all so amusing.
> To think I did all that,
> And may I say not in a shy way. Oh no, oh no, not me.
> I did it my way!'

Curtain

PROPS

On stage   A door

Two free standing hospital signs with arrows, first with words, 'PATHOLOGY/MORGUE', second with, 'DOMESTICS/STAFF TOILETS'

Four straight-backed chairs in a row

Table with an untidy assortment of magazines

Three chairs around table

Personal   For **Frank**, blue handkerchief, *(off)* three plastic beakers of tea/coffee, biscuits

For **Hilda**, shopping bag, biro, newspaper

For **Cleaning Lady**, large-headed sweeping brush, an electric floor polisher, damp cleaning cloth, shopping bag, biro, ghetto blaster

SOUND EFFECTS

Please note that permission from **Jasper Publishing** to perform this play **does not** include permission to use copyright songs and music suggested here. Performers are urged to consult the Performing Right Society Ltd., 29-33 Berners St, London W1P 4AA

Cue 1	Ambulance siren
Cue 2	'Dem bones, dem bones, dem dry bones'
Cue 3	'Ko-Ko's Song' from 'Trio and Chorus', The Mikado, Gilbert and Sullivan
Cue 4	The Sergeant's Song', Act 2, Pirates of Penzance, Gilbert and Sullivan
Cue 5	'Pooh-Bah's Song' from 'Trio and Chorus' Act 2, The Mikado, Gilbert and Sullivan
Cue 6	'John Brown's Body Lies A-Mouldering In The Grave'
Cue 7	'Right Said Fred' Music - Ted Dicks, Words - Myles Rudge
Cue 8	Theme Music from film 'Jaws'
Cue 9	'My Way' Lyrics - Paul Anka